D1266012

The Southeast

DANA MEACHEN RAU

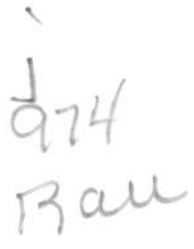

Children's Press®
An Imprint of Scholastic Inc.
New York Toronto London Auckland Sydney
Mexico City New Delhi Hong Kong
Danbury, Connecticut

Front cover, center: Forsyth Park fountain in Savannah, Georgia
Front cover, top right: Florida oranges
Front cover, bottom left: House in historic Charleston, South Carolina

Content Consultant
James Wolfinger, PhD
Associate Professor
DePaul University
Chicago, Illinois

Library of Congress Cataloging-in-Publication Data

Rau, Dana Meachen, 1971–
The Southeast/by Dana Meachen Rau.
p. cm.—(A true book)
Includes bibliographical references and index.
ISBN-13: 978-0-531-24852-2 (lib. bdg.) ISBN-10: 0-531-24852-6 (lib. bdg.)
ISBN-13: 978-0-531-28327-1 (pbk.) ISBN-10: 0-531-28327-5 (pbk.)
1. Southern States—Juvenile literature. I. Title. II. Series.
F209.3.R38 2012
975—dc23 2011031704

Printed in China 62

1 2 3 4 5 6 7 8 9 10 R 21 20 19 18 17 16 15 14 13 12

Find the Truth!

Everything you are about to read is true ***except*** for one of the sentences on this page.

Which one is **TRUE**?

T or F Florida grows more oranges than any other state.

T or F America's first permanent English colony was founded in Georgia.

Find the answers in this book.

Contents

1 Mountains, Coasts, and in Between

What is unique about the Southeast's landforms? 7

2 History of the Southeast

How has the Southeast changed over time? 15

Artists and Inventors of the Southeast. 21

3 People of the Southeast

Who lives in the Southeast? 23

THE BIG TRUTH!

Animals of the Southeast

What animals make their homes in the Southeast? 28

North river otter

Mardi Gras in New Orleans

4 Resources and Economy

How does the Southeast make use of its resources? **31**

5 Disaster in the Gulf

What challenges does the Southeast face? **39**

True Statistics **43**

Resources **44**

Important Words **46**

Index **47**

About the Author **48**

All horses in the Kentucky Derby are three years old.

N
W
E
S
0 miles 200
0 km 200
LEGEND
National capital
State capitals
Major cities
Ohio R.
WEST VIRGINIA
Washington, DC
VIRGINIA
Charleston
Richmond
Louisville
Frankfort
KENTUCKY
Virginia Beach
Great Smoky Mtns.
Appalachian Mountains
Raleigh
Nashville
NORTH CAROLINA
TENNESSEE
Charlotte
Memphis
ARKANSAS
Mississippi River
SOUTH CAROLINA
Columbia
Little Rock
MISSISSIPPI
Atlanta
ALABAMA
GEORGIA
Jackson
Montgomery
Savannah
LOUISIANA
ATLANTIC OCEAN
Mobile
Jacksonville
Baton Rouge
Tallahassee
New Orleans
FLORIDA
Orlando
Gulf of Mexico
Miami
The United States
Everglades
BAHAMAS

CHAPTER 1

Mountains, Coasts, and in Between

The Southeast region is made up of 12 states. These states include Alabama, Arkansas, Florida, Georgia, Kentucky, Louisiana, Mississippi, North Carolina, South Carolina, Tennessee, Virginia, and West Virginia. This region has a very long coastline. Five of the states border the Atlantic Ocean. Four sit on the **Gulf** of Mexico. Florida juts out into the ocean. This **peninsula** is surrounded by water on three sides. West Virginia, Kentucky, Tennessee, and Arkansas are **landlocked** by other U.S. states.

Look at the Land

The Southeast has a variety of landforms. The high land of the Appalachian **plateau** extends from north to south in the region. Some of the mountain ranges in the Appalachian system include the Allegheny, the Cumberland, and the Great Smoky Mountains. Early in U.S. history, the mountains were a natural barrier between eastern communities and the unexplored West. In 1775, **pioneers** started crossing the mountains through the Cumberland Gap. Their efforts opened the way for further expansion.

The Appalachian Mountains stretch from Alabama all the way into Canada.

The Mississippi River begins at Lake Itasca in Minnesota.

The Mississippi River is an important shipping route.

The Mississippi River runs through the Southeast. This mighty river is the second longest in the United States. The soil around the **delta**, where the river empties into the Gulf of Mexico, is ideal for farming.

The region's long coastline provides southeasterners access to the sea for fishing and shipping. Flat, sandy beaches on these coastal plains attract many tourists during the year.

Hurricanes form over the ocean before they hit land.

Hurricane Irene caused serious flooding in towns such as Manteo, North Carolina.

Climate

The Southeast has a humid subtropical climate. Summers are long and hot. The air is humid and wet. Ocean and gulf breezes help cool off coastal areas. But dangerous hurricanes blowing in from the water can cause damage. In 2011, Hurricane Irene caused almost $200 million in damages in North Carolina.

Winters are cool and mild. **Precipitation** usually falls in the form of rain. Higher areas such as the mountains get some snowfall.

Crops grow well in the region's hot, humid weather, so farms cover the Southeast. The long summers also mean a long growing season. This turns into higher profits for farmers. However, southeastern farmers sometimes experience **drought**. Their crops don't get enough water. If winter is colder than expected, frost can hurt crops as well.

The Southeast has a strong agricultural economy.

Unique Plant Life

The climate of the Southeast makes it the perfect home for more plant life than crops. The magnolia tree, with its big white flowers, blooms for a long season. The bald cypress tree is also an interesting sight. These trees can grow in standing water. They flourish in the slow-moving streams called bayous in the marshes of Louisiana. Spanish moss hangs down from the branches.

Bald cypress trees can grow to be 150 feet (46 meters) tall.

Alligators are a common sight in the Florida Everglades.

The Everglades, a swampy region in subtropical Florida, has many kinds of plants and animals. The roots of mangrove trees reach down into the shallow water. These roots provide safe shelters for water wildlife, such as snook, shrimp, and crabs. Above the water, wood storks and other waterbirds nest among the mangroves. They eat the water animals sheltering nearby. The trees also help keep the coast from being worn away by harsh gulf storms.

More settlers came to the Southeast as Virginia had success with tobacco crops.

CHAPTER 2

History of the Southeast

Settlers looking for riches arrived at present-day Virginia in 1607. They founded Jamestown, the first permanent English settlement in America. The English had a rough time. Many colonists died from disease, harsh weather, and lack of food.

Then the settlers discovered that tobacco grew well in the soil. Farmers could send the tobacco to England for a large profit. The colony's wealth and success quickly grew. Agriculture, or farming, is still important to southeasterners today.

Colonies Become States

English colonists also settled in Georgia and Carolina. Carolina later split into two colonies called North Carolina and South Carolina. Colonists farmed tobacco, rice, and indigo on large farms called plantations. People in Africa were captured and forced to come to the Southeast. There, they planted and harvested the colonists' crops.

In the late 1700s, the colonists defeated Britain in the Revolutionary War. The former English colonies came together to form a new country called the United States.

Slaves provided almost all of the labor on large plantations.

Florida was a Spanish colony before joining the United States in 1845.

The cotton gin brought major changes to southeastern agriculture.

The Cotton Boom

After the war, farmers needed a new crop. Soil that had grown nothing but tobacco for years could no longer support tobacco crops. Cotton, which also grew well in the southeastern climate, was difficult to harvest. But Eli Whitney's development of the cotton gin in 1793 changed that. This machine quickly separated the plant's soft fibers from its seeds. Harvesting cotton became faster and easier. Cotton farming soon stretched from parts of Virginia into Texas.

The northern and southern United States disagreed on many issues, especially slavery. The South's agricultural success depended on enslaved workers. To protect their way of life, some southern states **seceded** from the United States. They formed the Confederate States of America.

The North did not want the South to leave the country. The two sides fought the American Civil War from 1861 to 1865. The North won, and President Abraham Lincoln freed the slaves.

Southeastern Timeline

1607

The first English colony settles in Jamestown, Virginia.

1775–1783

The American colonies and Britain fight in the Revolutionary War.

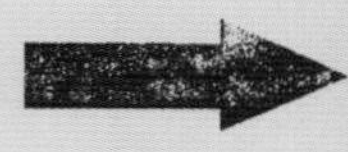

Rebuilding After the War

Much of the Southeast had been damaged during the war. Southeasterners had to rebuild. They also needed to find ways to farm without using enslaved people. Many wealthy planters used **sharecropping**. They loaned plots of land to former slaves and other small farmers. In return, the planters received a share of the profits. But profits were often small, and the sharecroppers sometimes could not afford to pay the wealthy planters. As a result, many sharecroppers lived in poor conditions.

1793

Eli Whitney's invention of the cotton gin boosts the southern economy.

1861–1865

The North and South fight in the American Civil War.

1964

The Civil Rights Act is passed, stating that public places could no longer be segregated.

Martin Luther King Jr. believed that the equal rights debate could be solved peacefully.

Meanwhile, new laws gave African Americans rights, including voting and receiving an education. But many states refused to follow these laws. Southeastern states practiced **segregation**. Black and white Americans were kept separate in public places. African Americans were still treated unfairly.

Martin Luther King Jr. was a minister who was born in Atlanta, Georgia. He and other people led the civil rights movement in the 1950s and 1960s. They called for everyone to be treated equally. Slowly, laws began changing to better protect the rights of African Americans.

Artists and Inventors of the Southeast

Louis Armstrong

Louis Armstrong (1901–1971) was a jazz musician who played the cornet and trumpet, and was also a singer. He was born in Louisiana.

Cynthia Rylant (1954–) is a Newbery award-winning children's author who has written many stories about life in the Appalachian Mountains. She was born in Virginia and raised in West Virginia. She is the author of the very popular Henry and Mudge series.

Beulah Henry (1887–1973) has been credited with more than 100 inventions, including improvements to typewriters, toys, and sewing machines. She was born in Tennessee.

Architecture in the French Quarter is influenced by the Cajuns who settled there.

CHAPTER 3

People of the Southeast

The Southeast includes a variety of cultures. Some are unique to the region. In Louisiana, Cajuns and Creoles speak a combination of French and other languages. Their cooking uses the area's resources, including seafood and spices. Gumbo and jambalaya are popular dishes. Rice is another common ingredient. It grows in the Southeast's warm, wet climate.

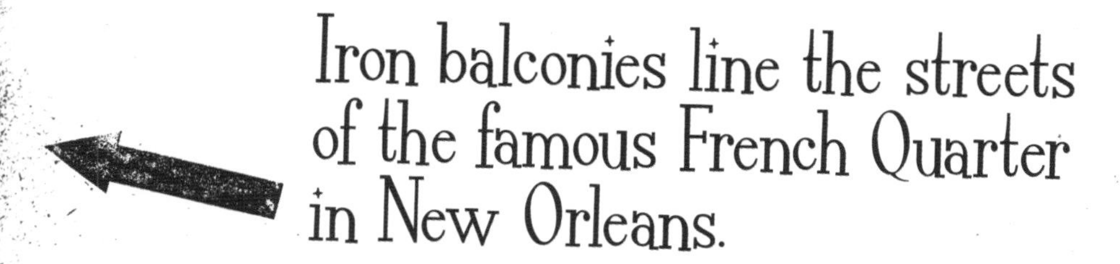

Iron balconies line the streets of the famous French Quarter in New Orleans.

An Excellent Education

The Southeast has more than 100 historically black colleges and universities, more than any other region in the United States. Most of these schools were built after the Civil War to provide higher education to African Americans. They continue to educate students of all backgrounds. Their graduates include businessperson Oprah Winfrey, Supreme Court justice Thurgood Marshall, educator Booker T. Washington, and actor Samuel L. Jackson.

Samuel L. Jackson graduated from Morehouse College, a men's college in Atlanta, Georgia.

More African American men have earned bachelor's degrees from Morehouse College than any other U.S. school.

Miami's Little Havana is a neighborhood made up mainly of Cuban Americans.

Cultural Roots and New Visitors

Parts of Florida are heavily influenced by Hispanic culture. Miami has a large Hispanic population. Most of the people came from Cuba, an island off the coast. Hispanic traditions are found in Miami's music, food, and language.

Older people from other U.S. states often retire and move to Florida to enjoy the yearlong sunshine and beautiful weather. As a result, Florida has many health and service jobs at medical centers and retirement homes. These workers care for the state's older residents.

Atlanta is home to more than 400,000 people.

Atlanta was destroyed by fire during the Civil War in 1864.

Keeping Cool

Most people in the Southeast live in and near cities. Atlanta, the largest city and capital of Georgia, and its suburbs hold half of all of Georgia's population. In the summer, Southeastern cities get hot. The Centennial Olympic Park in Atlanta is a great place to cool off. People enjoy playing in the water of these large public fountains in the shape of the Olympic Rings.

The Nation's Capital

Washington, D.C., is not a state. It's a district. But it is often considered part of the Southeast region. Washington, D.C., is home to the offices of the U.S. government. The nation's first president, George Washington, chose to place the city here on the Potomac River in 1791. The city was built with organized rows of streets, with the U.S. Capitol in the center.

Many Americans travel to Washington, D.C., to visit the U.S. Capitol and other important buildings and monuments.

Animals of the Southeast

Many animals live in the coastal plains of the Southeast.

Northern river otters are playful water mammals. Their bodies are designed for swimming. They have webbed toes, waterproof fur, and long, thin bodies. River otters are rare in some parts of the United States. But they are often found in the southeastern region.

American alligators are the largest reptiles in North America. They are good hunters. They have strong jaws for eating fish, frogs, turtles, snakes, mammals, and birds. They live in marshes, swamps, and bayous.

White ibis are bright white birds. They wade along shores or in marshes on their long, red legs. They search for fish, frogs, and insects with their long, red, curved bills. Ibis often live in groups called colonies.

Factories in North Carolina produce jet engines for large passenger planes.

CHAPTER 4

Resources and Economy

The people of the Southeast hold a variety of jobs. Some manufacture goods, such as chemicals, transportation equipment, and electronics. There are large food and beverage companies in this region, too. Shipping companies are located near ports along the Gulf and the Atlantic. Many people work in restaurants, hotels, and other businesses that provide services. As it has been throughout history, agriculture is a vital part of the Southeast's economy.

More than half of the world's people eat rice as a regular part of their diets.

Rice requires very wet conditions to grow.

Farming

The Mississippi delta and other river valleys provide a rich base for agriculture. The Native American groups living in the region first farmed along the river valleys. The fertile southeastern soil and the warm, wet climate are still ideal conditions for farming. Today, farmers grow cotton, tobacco, soybeans, and corn. Arkansas's location on the delta yields more rice than any other U.S. state.

Florida is called the Sunshine State. Its hot, sunny weather makes it the perfect place to grow citrus fruits. Florida grows more oranges, grapefruits, and tangerines than any other state. Most of the oranges are squeezed to make orange juice.

But Florida isn't always sunny. When the weather becomes unexpectedly cold, frost can destroy the fruit. Farmers sometimes use heaters or sprinklers to keep the fruit from freezing.

Harvest season is a busy time of year for citrus growers in Florida.

Mining

The land of the Appalachian plateau is not very suitable for farming. So people in this area looked to the mountains for resources. West Virginia sits above a large natural supply of coal. Miners also dig for coal in Kentucky, Virginia, and Tennessee. Throughout the nation's history, this coal has provided fuel for industries, for heating, and to generate electricity.

Coal miners often work in dark, very tight spaces.

Oil is one of the most important natural resources in the world.

Closer to the Gulf, oil and natural gas are trapped deep underground. People reach these energy resources by drilling wells on land and under the Gulf waters.

In 2010, a disaster on an oil rig in the Gulf poured millions of gallons of oil into the ocean. The fishing industry relies on these waters for shrimp, crabs, oysters, and clams. This industry is still recovering from the damage to the ocean and to the health of its wildlife.

Millions of people travel to Florida every year to visit the state's many exciting amusement parks.

Welcoming Visitors

The tourist industry employs many people in the Southeast. Florida's amusement parks and beaches are popular vacation spots. Tourists also visit Washington, D.C. The city has many museums and memorials. The town of Williamsburg, Virginia, is nearby. Many of its historic sites have been re-created, so that visitors can see what life was like long ago.

The Kentucky Derby

Horse farms in the bluegrass region of Kentucky raise thoroughbreds. These horses are built to race.

The Kentucky Derby is held every May. This 1.25-mile (2 kilometer) race is held at Churchill Downs in Louisville, Kentucky. The oval track first opened in 1875. Races have been held there every year since. Each horse has an owner, a trainer, and a jockey. The jockey rides the horse across the finish line—hopefully in first place!

Strong winds were just one of the many problems brought on by Hurricane Katrina.

CHAPTER 5

Disaster in the Gulf

In August 2005, a hurricane formed in the Caribbean Sea and was headed toward the southeastern United States. First, it hit Florida. Next it traveled over the Gulf. The winds grew stronger. Then it struck Louisiana and Mississippi.

Some parts of the city of New Orleans, Louisiana, are below sea level. **Levees** built along waterways usually keep water from flooding the land. But they couldn't keep back the rising water brought by Hurricane Katrina.

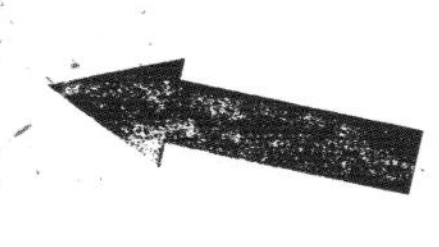

Atlantic hurricanes are most common in August and September.

Destruction

Parts of the levees broke, and most of New Orleans flooded. People climbed onto rooftops to escape the rising waters. The hurricane completely destroyed parts of the city, including homes and schools. Many people died.

Mississippi was hit hard, too. All over the region, people's homes and belongings were completely destroyed. Hurricanes are one of the challenges of living in this area. But Hurricane Katrina was one of the worst storms in U.S. history.

Hurricane Katrina was one of the most destructive natural disasters ever to hit the United States.

Volunteers traveled to New Orleans from around the country to help rebuild.

Rebuilding

Rebuilding took lots of time and money. To prevent such a large disaster from happening again, the U.S. Army Corps of Engineers set to work rebuilding levees and floodwalls. The new levees are taller than the old ones. This reduces the chance of water pouring over the top. New floodwalls reach much deeper into the ground. This makes them more stable and less likely to break.

People are once again traveling to New Orleans to enjoy the parades and festivals that the city is known for.

The population of New Orleans is not as large as it was before the storm. But many people have been coming back. Construction businesses, government workers, and volunteers have helped rebuild neighborhoods and businesses. Organizations provide money to give business owners, homeless people, and artists a new start. As the city rebuilds, visitors have returned to New Orleans, too. They come to see a part of a region with a history of strength, culture, and unique beauty. ★

True Statistics

Number of states in the region: 12

Major rivers of the region: Mississippi, Savannah, Tennessee

Major mountain ranges of the region: Appalachian Mountains

Climate: Humid subtropical, humid continental

Largest cities: Jacksonville, MS; Charlotte, WV; Memphis, TN

Products: Cotton, rice, sugarcane, nuts, fruits, livestock, seafood, coal, oil, natural gas

Borders of the region:

- **North:** Northeast and Midwest regions
- **East:** Atlantic Ocean
- **South:** Gulf of Mexico
- **West:** Southwest region

Did you find the truth?

T Florida grows more oranges than any other state.

F America's first permanent English colony was founded in Georgia.

Resources

Books

Elish, Dan. *Louis Armstrong and the Jazz Age*. New York: Children's Press, 2008.

Gunderson, Jessica. *Eli Whitney and the Cotton Gin*. Mankato, MN: Capstone, 2007.

January, Brendan F. *The Jamestown Colony*. Minneapolis: Compass Point Books, 2001.

Johnson, Robin. *The Mississippi: America's Mighty River*. New York: Crabtree Publishing, 2009.

Maynard, Charles W. *The Appalachians*. New York: PowerKids Press, 2004.

Miller, Millie, and Cyndi Nelson. *The United States of America: A State-by-State Guide*. New York: Scholastic Reference, 2006.

Rau, Dana Meachen. *North America*. Chanhassen, MN: The Child's World, 2004.

Santella, Andrew. *Daniel Boone and the Cumberland Gap*. Danbury, CT: Children's Press, 2007.

Skog, Jason Maurice. *The Civil Rights Act of 1964*. Minneapolis: Compass Point Books, 2007.

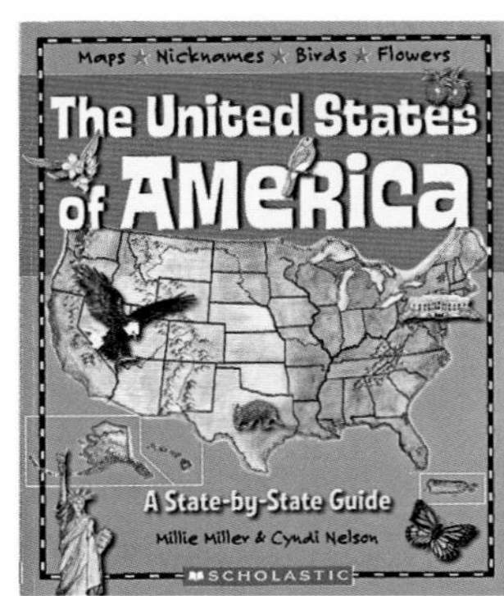

Organizations and Web Sites

Smithsonian National Museum of American History

http://americanhistory.si.edu

Check out this site to see exhibits and learn about the growth of America.

U.S. Census 2010 Interactive Population Map

http://2010.census.gov/2010census/popmap

Learn about the populations of the states with this interactive map.

Places to Visit

Colonial Williamsburg

101 Visitor Center Drive
Williamsburg, VA 23185
(800) 447-8679
www.colonialwilliamsburg.com

Travel back to colonial times. Tour homes, see museums, and find out about life in early America.

Everglades National Park

40001 State Road 9336
Homestead, FL 33034
(305) 242-7700
www.nps.gov/ever

See the animals and plants of this unique habitat of Florida's shores.

Visit this Scholastic web site for more information on the U.S. Southeast:

www.factsfornow.scholastic.com

Important Words

delta (DEL-tuh) — an area of land shaped like a triangle where a river enters the sea

drought (DROUT) — a long period without rain

gulf (GUHLF) — a large area of sea that is partly surrounded by land

landlocked (LAND-lahkt) — surrounded by land on all sides

levees (LEV-eez) — banks built up near a river to prevent flooding

peninsula (puh-NIN-suh-luh) — a piece of land that sticks out from a larger landmass and is almost completely surrounded by water

pioneers (pye-uh-NEERZ) — people who explore unknown territory and settle there

plateau (pla-TOH) — area of high, flat land

precipitation (pri-sip-i-TAY-shuhn) — the falling of water from the sky in the form of rain, sleet, hail, or snow

seceded (si-SEED-id) — formally withdrew from a group or organization

segregation (seg-ri-GAY-shuhn) — the act or practice of keeping people or groups apart

sharecropping (SHAIR-crop-ing) — farming land that belongs to another person in return for a share of the profits

Index

Page numbers in **bold** indicate illustrations

African Americans, **16**, 18, 19, **20**, **24**
Alabama, 7
American Civil War, 18, **19**, 24, 26
animals, **13**, **28–29**, 35
Appalachian Mountains, **8**, 21
Arkansas, 7, 32
Atlanta, Georgia, 20, **24**, **26**
Atlantic Ocean, 7, 31, **38**

civil rights movement, 19, **20**
climate, **10**–11, 12, 13, 17, 23, 26, 32, 33, **38**, 39, **40**
coastline, 7, 9, 10, 13, 25, 28

economy, **11**, 15, **19**, 31
education, 20, **24**

farming, 9, **11**, 15, **16**, **17**, 18, **19**, 23, **32–33**, 37
fishing, 9, 35
flooding, **10**, 39, **40**, 41
Florida, 7, **13**, 17, **25**, **33**, **36**, 39
food, 15, 23, 25, 31

Georgia, 7, 16, 20, **24**, 26
Gulf of Mexico, 7, 9, 10, 13, 31, 35, 39

hurricanes, **10**, **38**, 39, **40**

industries, **30**, 31, 34, 35, **36**

jobs, 25, **30**, 31, **34**, 42

Kentucky, 7, 34, **37**

languages, 23, 25
Louisiana, 7, 12, 21, **22**, 39, 40, **41–42**

map, **6**
Miami, Florida, **25**
mining, **34–35**
Mississippi, 7, 39, 40
mountains, **8**, 10, 21, 34

Native Americans, 32
New Orleans, Louisiana, **22**, 39, 40, **41–42**
North Carolina, 7, **10**, 16, **30**

oil industry, **35**

plants, **12**–13, 17
plateaus, 8, 34
populations, 25, **26**, 42

Revolutionary War, 16, **18**
rice, 16, 23, **32**

settlers, 8, **14**, 15, 16, **18**
slavery, **16**, 18, 19
South Carolina, 7, 16

Tennessee, 7, 21, 34
Texas, 17
timeline, **18–19**
tourism, 9, **36**, **42**
transportation, **9**, **30**, 31

U.S. Capitol, **27**

Virginia, 7, **14**, 15, 17, **18**, 21, 34, 36

Washington, D.C., **27**, 36
West Virginia, 7, 21, 34

About the Author

Dana Meachen Rau is the author of more than 300 books for children. A graduate of Trinity College in Hartford, Connecticut, she has written fiction and nonfiction titles including early readers and books on science, history, cooking, and many other topics that interest her. She especially loves to write books that take her to other places, even when she doesn't have time for a vacation. Dana lives with her family in Burlington, Connecticut. To learn more about her books, please visit *www.danameachenrau.com*.